Are We There Yet?

How can visits to other times and other places make our lives better?

page 4

page 18

READING ACROSS TEXTS

Related Readings and Projects

Lengths of Time

By Phyllis McGinley

Time is peculiar
And hardly exact.
Though minutes are minutes,
You'll find for a fact
(As the older you get
And the bigger you grow)
That time can
Hurrylikethis
or plod, plod, slow.

Waiting for your dinner when you're hungry?
Down with the sniffles in your bed?
Notice how an hour crawls along and crawls along
Like a snail with his house upon his head.

But when you are starting
A game in the park,
It's morning,
It's noon,
And suddenly it's dark.
And hours like seconds
Rush blurringly by,
Whoosh!
Like a plane in the sky.

Time Train

In "Lengths of Time," minutes seem to speed up or slow down. It depends on how people use their time. How have people used their time at different periods of history? What can we learn from thinking about time and how people use it?

Make a Time Train to compare and contrast the use of time in the past, the present, and the future.

Gather Information

1. Collect three shoeboxes with lids. Connect the boxes to form a three-boxcar train. Label the boxes Past, Present, and Future.

2. Collect items that show how you spend your time today. For example, if you play soccer, you could use a water bottle or shin guard.

3. Collect items that show how your parents and grandparents spent their time when they were your age. Interview them to find out.

4. Think about the future. Collect items that show how your children might spend their time when they grow to be your age. Ask friends and relatives for ideas.

5. Write short explanations for each item on index cards.

Organize and Draw Conclusions

6. Place the items in the box where they belong.

7. Make notes on how the items in one box are similar to and different from the items in the other boxes.

Write and Present

8. Use your notes to write an explanation of how time has been used in the past, the present, and the future. Then present your time train to the class. You might want to give a speech based on your written explanation.

Grandma Buffalo, May, *and Me*

By Carol Curtis Stilz   Illustrated by Constance R. Bergum

As darkness crept over our campsite, Mama lit a lantern whose two tiny baskets made white light. I took Grandma's leather-covered photo album from our bag, opening it to our family tree.

Mama, Gray Bear, and I are going to visit my Montana grandma. Mama says we are on an adventure, creating a story for the branch that is ours.

"Mama, tell me again about our family tree."

"The roots of a family tree grow deep in time, Poppy. Each branch is a story of the people in our family who lived before us. Our album shows photographs of some relatives and tells part of their stories."

I named these relatives "the greats": great-grandparents, great-great-grandparents, and great-aunts and -uncles. They have old-fashioned names like Melvin, Harriet, Zillah, and Asahel.

I searched for a picture of May, who looked just like me.

"Tell me again about Great-Grandma May."

"May was my grandmother," Mama said. "When she was young, her wavy hair was the color of poppies and her eyes were green as moss. Her laugh sounded like the spring we heard today bubbling from the earth. When May was your age, she learned to catch fish, plant a garden, and feed buffalo."

"Tell me again about the buffalo."

"My great-uncle told of a man named Samuel Walking Coyote, who brought buffalo to the Flathead and Mission valleys in Montana. Long ago, four baby buffalo followed him from the plains, where buffalo were hunted, to these valleys, where they were protected. The baby buffalo grew

up and had calves of their own. The buffalo May fed were related to those baby buffalo."

"Will we see buffalo?"

"I hope so. Buffalo don't roam free now, but they aren't tame like cows. They're wild animals living in parks and on ranches. Some descendants of May's buffalo live near Grandma. They are probably fast asleep, and it's our bedtime too."

In the dark I listened for coyotes like those that sang May to sleep. I heard one call far away as I watched the moon rise. That night I dreamed of buffalo, May, and me in Montana.

The next morning we drove down the mountainside, stopping beside a stream.

Mama said, "Let's see if the fish are biting."

She tied a hook covered with soft fur to my line. The fur hid the hook and looked like the bugs on the water below. I held my new fly rod and Mama wrapped her hand around mine.

"Move your hand just past your shoulder, then bring your arm forward quickly."

On my first try, the hook caught on the bush behind me. On my second try, the line tangled in the grass. The third time, my line swished past my ear and my fly hit the water. Than Mama cast. Her line sang in the air before her fly touched the stream.

Suddenly I felt a tug.

Mama helped me reel in my line. A silvery fish flip-flopped from the end. I stroked its slippery body.

"Can we let it go? This fish is so big and sparkly!"

Mama slipped the fish off the hook. I helped her rock it gently back and forth underwater so it could breathe. It wiggled. When we opened our hands, it darted away.

After lunch we drove through wheat fields, past tall, round towers called silos. We drove down a dusty road toward a sign that read: Buffalo Bridge. I didn't see any buffalo. Neither did Gray Bear.

"Where are the buffalo?" I asked.

"Long ago, buffalo lived here," Mama said. "Now let's find May's place."

We stopped at a big, white farmhouse surrounded by poppies. We knocked on the door and introduced ourselves to the woman inside. Mama had written to ask if we could visit, explaining that May lived there when she was my age.

The woman smiled, gave me a sack, and said, "You're welcome to gather apples from May's McIntosh trees." We followed her out back.

Mama gave me a boost into a tree. Higher and higher I climbed, under an umbrella of green leaves and red apples, imagining May gathering apples too. I searched for buffalo but didn't see any. Instead I saw faraway farmhouses, golden grass, and a rainbow of flowers.

When I climbed down, the woman gave me two surprises. The first was a sealed envelope. She said, "I save the seeds from May's poppies. Plant them and next spring you'll have flowers the color of your hair."

The second surprise was a carefully wrapped twig. "This cutting from May's apple tree will root if you put it in rich soil. When its roots grow strong, plant it outside. With cuttings from May's trees, we grew the trees you see now."

"Thanks! Now I'll have my own little McIntosh tree."

"Perhaps someday your daughter will pick apples from your tree, and you can tell her the story of Great-Grandma May," Mama said. "Now let's find buffalo."

Back in the car, we drove along straight, dusty roads. I was hungry, so I took three apples from the sack. I gave one to Mama. Gray Bear wasn't hungry, so I stuffed his apple in my pocket.

I saw a sign that read: Buffalo Crossing.

"Are the buffalo here?" I asked.

"I hope so. Grandma knows the man who runs this ranch."

We stopped at a big log house, stepped up on the porch, and knocked on the door. The man who answered told us, "Buffalo are shy and stay away from folks they don't know. Still, you may see them on the hillsides, under trees, or near the river."

"My great-grandma May fed buffalo when she was my age, and I want to feed buffalo too."

The man's forehead wrinkled while he thought. "There is only one buffalo gentle enough to feed. Grandma Buffalo. She's my oldest, seventy-four in buffalo years. That's twenty of our years. I bottle-fed her as a baby, and she will eat from people's hands." As Mama drove, she said, "Poppy, watch for buffalo."

"Look! Is that one?" I asked.

Our car inched along so we wouldn't scare the buffalo, but it moved farther and farther away until it disappeared. I searched the hillsides, watched the bushes and stared into shadows beneath the trees. I didn't see any more buffalo, but I felt them staring at me.

"They must be hiding," I said.

Soon we would be leaving the ranch. I held my breath, hoping we would find Grandma Buffalo.

"Stop!" I shouted.

Mama parked our car. This buffalo was big and brown, with a hump and horns. We walked on short grass that crunched with every step. The buffalo ambled through long grass, quiet as a whisper.

We followed, strolling toward a woman waiting near the fence.

"Hi," she said. "I'm Mary Elizabeth Hawk. I visit Grandma Buffalo whenever I can. My family has raised buffalo since my ancestor Walking Coyote first brought them to this valley."

"I know about Walking Coyote," I said. "Are you related to him?"

"Yes, I am, just as Grandma Buffalo is related to the buffalo he brought with him."

"My great-grandma May fed buffalo when she was my age, and I want to feed buffalo too."

"Grandma Buffalo has four stomachs, so you won't spoil her appetite. She is very strong, but gentle."

I turned to Grandma Buffalo. A short, woolly coat covered her back. A shaggy mane covered her head and shoulders. Gray Bear thought Grandma Buffalo needed a haircut. I stroked her long, soft mane. Then I reached for Gray Bear's apple in my pocket.

"Grandma Buffalo, this apple is from Great-Grandma May's McIntosh tree."

Grandma Buffalo looked at me with big chocolate-drop eyes. She wrapped her long, purplish black tongue around the apple. Her tongue tickled. She rubbed her head against my hand, chewed, and swallowed. A soft sound in her throat said, "Thank you."

Mama laughed.

"She's talking to you, Poppy. Maybe her great-great-great-grandmother told her of a little girl with wavy hair the color of poppies who fed her apples long ago."

I gently patted Grandma Buffalo. "Do you remember?"

Later, Mama lit the lantern. She said, "Tomorrow night we'll see Grandma and sleep in her house."

I took Grandma's leather-covered photo album from our bag. Gray Bear and I turned its yellowed pages, searching for May's picture.

I imagined May feeding apples from her tree to a buffalo who lived long ago. I heard her buffalo rumble its thanks.

"Does Grandma know my story is like Great-Grandma May's?"

"What will you tell her?"

"Great-Grandma May and I shared an adventure. We learned to catch fish, plant a garden, and feed buffalo. Today I picked apples from her tree. Soon I will plant my twig and watch its roots grow strong. Someday I will pick apples from my McIntosh tree."

I touched the little branch of our family tree where my name was written. Then I said, "The roots of my family grow deep in time, just like Grandma Buffalo's."

What a Character!

When Mama tells Poppy about Grandma May, she uses interesting language:

"When she was young, her wavy hair was the color of poppies and her eyes were green *as* moss. Her laugh sounded *like* the spring we heard today bubbling from the earth."

When you read these words, how do you picture Grandma May? Mama uses *similes*—comparisons that use the word *like* or *as*.

Describe someone you know. Use interesting similes to help people picture that person in their minds.

What You Do

1. Choose a person to describe. Do not choose a classmate. Picture that person clearly in your mind.

2. Make a T-chart like the one below.

3. Use your chart to write your similes. Use *like* or *as* to compare the person to each item. Remember that you want to use words that help people picture and hear the person in their minds.

4. Draw a picture of the person to go with your similes.

Use What You Learn

5. Exchange your similes—but not the pictures—with a classmate. Read your classmate's similes and draw a detailed picture of the character. Have your classmate do the same with your similes. Then compare the results.

UNCLE BILL

Qualities	Comparisons
rough hands from working in the fields	sand
dark blue eyes	the deepest part of the ocean
low voice—scared me when I was little	a foghorn
gentle	a lamb

BRING ON THE BUFFALO!

In the book *Grandma Buffalo, May, and Me,* Poppy learns that buffalo are wild animals that stay away from folks they don't know. She also learns that they have four stomachs!

Here are some more facts about buffalo.

- There are several kinds of buffalo, also called oxen, that live in places all over the world.
- The black water buffalo lives in India. How did it get its name? It likes to soak in pools of water for hours and hours!
- In the Philippines, some wild buffalo are only 3 1/2 feet (107 centimeters) tall—about as tall as you are!
- The American buffalo is called a *bison.* About 100 years ago, fewer than 600 bison were left in the United States. The government passed laws to keep the bison from becoming extinct. Now the number of bison has risen to more than 15,000!
- The second largest city in New York is called Buffalo. There's even a football team named the Buffalo Bills! The buffalo nickel shows a buffalo on one side of the coin and the head of a Native American on the other.

During the 1800s, millions of buffalo in the United States began disappearing. By 1880 only a few thousand were left. Think about why they might have disappeared. Make a list of possible reasons. Then look up information on buffalo to see if you were right.

Cows
in the
Parlor

by Cynthia McFarland

Every day is a busy day on Clear Creek Farm. Winter, spring, summer, and fall, the cows on the dairy farm must be milked—twice a day, every day.

When the snow is deep in the fields, and when the hot summer sun shines down on the pastures, the cows need to be milked.

Even on holidays, Charlie Riddle, the farmer, must milk his cows. A dairy cow doesn't have a day off.

Maggie is a Jersey cow. Jerseys are always tan or brown. Some have white spots on their faces and bodies. They are friendly cows and like to be petted.

There are fifty cows on Clear Creek Farm, where Maggie lives. Fancy, Belle, Heather, and Sparkle are some of the other cows' names. It is not easy to think of names for fifty cows.

A tag with a number hangs from the chain around Maggie's neck. Another tag is attached to her ear. When a farmer has many cows, he needs a way to keep track of them. The numbers on the tags help him do this.

The neck chains jingle and rattle when the cows walk or shake their heads.

When the wind is blowing and it is raining or snowing, the cows stay inside the barn. The straw makes a cozy bed when it is cold outside.

When the weather is nice, the cows like to graze in the pasture. The sunshine is warm on Maggie's back as she rests after eating. In the spring and summer when the nights are warmer, the cows sleep outside in the cool grass.

A cow doesn't have top teeth at the front of her mouth as a horse, a dog, or a person does. Maggie has a very long, rough tongue. By wrapping it around the tall grass she can pull off a bite and then chew the grass with her strong back teeth.

In the summer, Mr. Riddle and the farm workers cut grass, dry it in the sun, and make it into bales of hay.

The cows will have hay to eat when the grass in the pasture is brown and dry in the winter.

But a cow needs more than grass and hay to make good milk. Charlie Riddle also makes feed from the corn that was planted in the spring.

Machines chop the whole cornstalk into small pieces.

Then the silo is filled with this chopped corn, which is called silage. The silo is very tall. It can hold enough silage to feed the farmer's cows for many months. When snow covers the cornfields, there will still be food for the cows in the silo.

The cows eat their silage at a long trough, called a bunk. Mr. Riddle uses a tractor and feed wagon to take the silage from the silo to the bunk, where the cows are waiting to eat. The cows moo when they see the tractor because they know that soon they will be fed.

Maggie and the other cows know when it is time to be milked because Charlie Riddle and the farm workers milk them at the same time every day. If the cows are out in the field, they start walking up to the barn gate at milking time.

Early in the morning, when most people are asleep in their warm beds, the cows are being milked. In the evening, when most people sit down to eat dinner, the cows must be milked again. At Clear Creek Farm, the Riddle family eats supper earlier in the afternoon, or after the evening milking is finished.

The parlor in a dairy barn is not a pretty living room. It is the room where the cows are milked.

When Maggie comes in to the parlor, her udder is firm and full of milk. She stands in a small pen, or stanchion, and the gates are closed so that she can't leave until she has been milked. Every time she is milked, her udder is cleaned and all the dirt is washed off.

Farmers used to milk their cows by hand into a bucket. That took a long time. Now there are automatic milking machines to make the job quicker and easier.

The milking machines don't hurt the cows. Suction from the machines gently pulls the milk from the cows' teats.

The milk runs through shiny silver pipes into a large tank. There the milk is kept cold until it is picked up by the milk hauler.

When the hauler comes, he pumps all the milk into his long tanker truck and takes it to the creamery. There the milk is made into butter, cheese, ice cream, and yogurt. It is also put into cartons so people can pour a glass to drink or have some on their cereal for breakfast. In one day a single cow can give enough milk to fill more than fifty glasses.

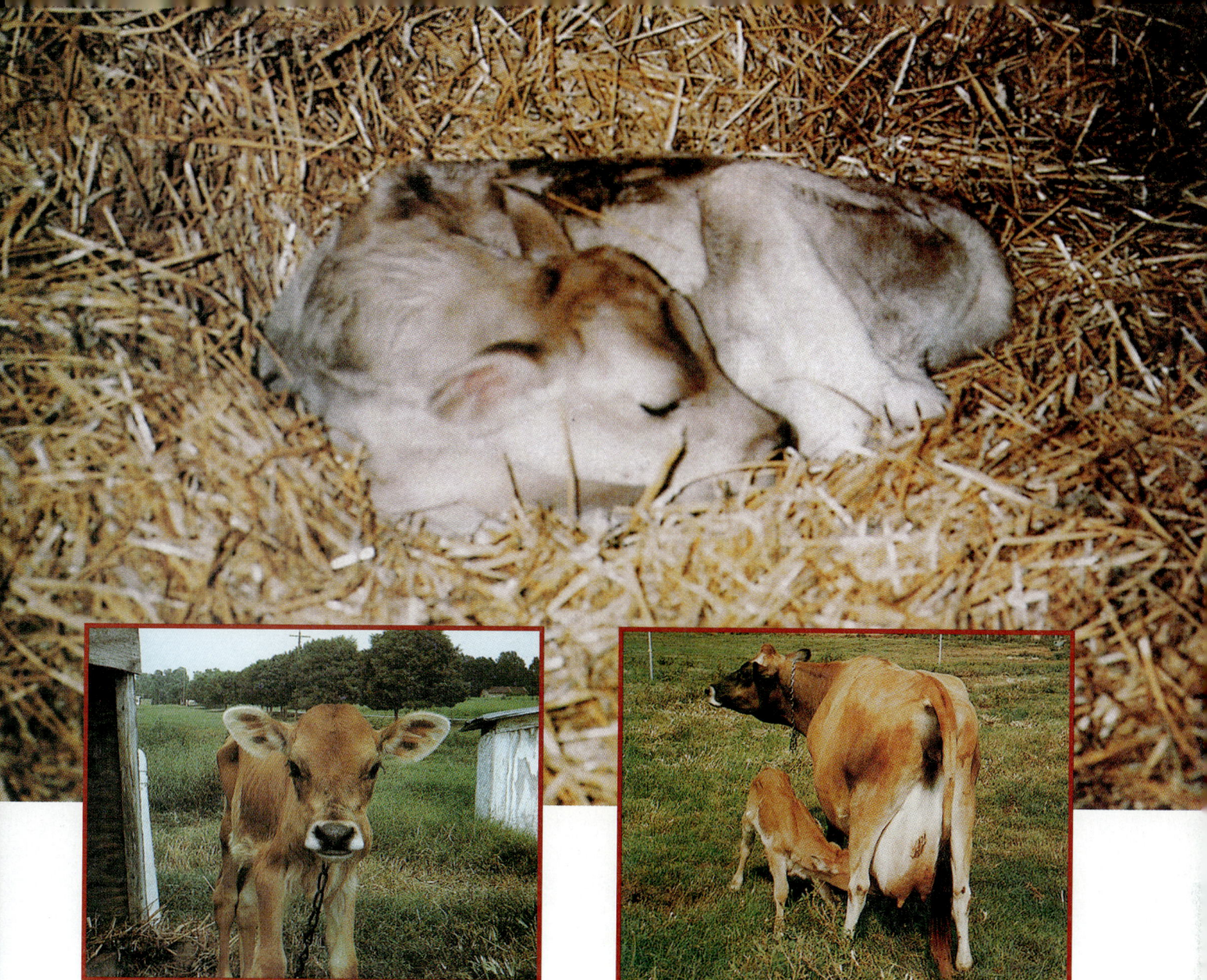

To keep making milk, a cow must have a baby every year. Cats and dogs have several babies at a time. A cow usually has only one.

Maggie has just had a calf. The calf is sweet and brown, with large dark eyes like a deer's.

The calf nurses from her mother. That first milk is very important to the baby. It is rich with extra vitamins to keep the newborn calf from getting sick.

After the calf has been with her a day, Maggie will go back into the milking herd. Her calf will live with all the other babies. Each calf has her own small pen bedded with fresh, sweet-smelling straw.

Mr. Riddle feeds them milk from a bottle, and they learn to eat grain from a bucket.

A calf is soft and warm and will suck on the farmer's finger, trying to find milk. She calls "maaa maaa" at feeding time.

Calves are frisky and like to play. After running and jumping, they take naps in the sunshine.

A female calf is called a heifer. A male calf is called a bull calf. Charlie Riddle keeps the heifers. Sometimes he sells the bull calves so another farmer can raise them.

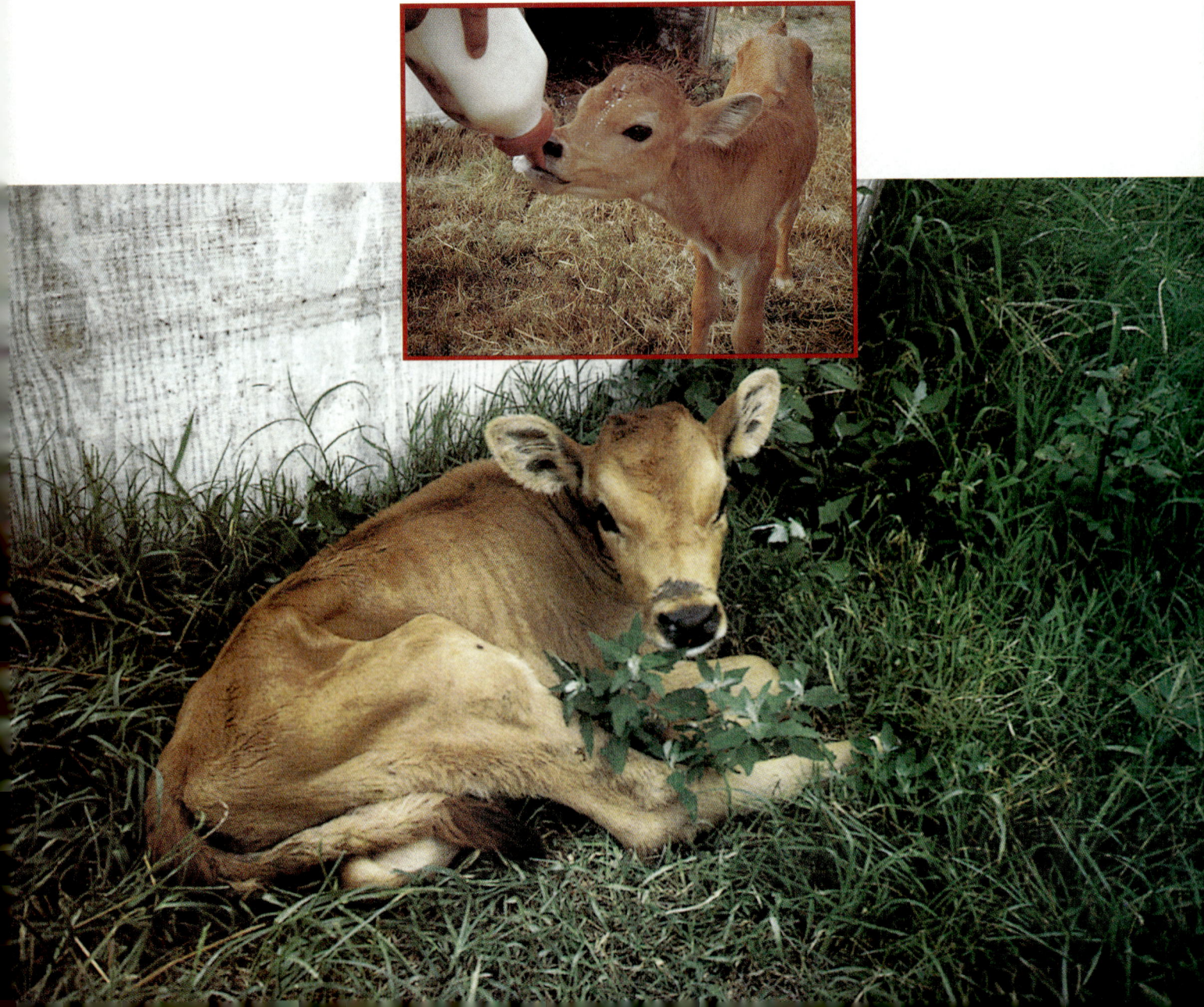

Maggie's calf is a heifer. In two years she will be old enough to be bred and have a baby of her own. After she calves, she will be called a cow and will become part of the milking herd just like her mother, Maggie.

After the evening milking, Mr. Riddle finishes his chores. When the parlor is clean, the milking machines and pipes are washed, and the cows are fed, his day's work is done.

The cows finish eating their dinner and lie down to sleep. Soon bright stars glitter in the night sky above the quiet, dark pastures.

When the morning sun comes up again, another busy day will already have begun on Clear Creek Farm.

Photo Essays

Cows in the Parlor is nonfiction—it's a true story about what happens on a dairy farm. The author uses more than words to tell about life on a dairy farm. She also shows you a collection of photos. These photos help you visualize what that life is like.

Nonfiction books that use many photos to help present information are called *photo essays*. In a photo essay, the words and photos are partners. The photos show you details that might be too long or complicated to write about. The photos make you an eyewitness to the events described in words.

The photos in a photo essay don't show everything that the words describe. They show details that the writer feels are important for her readers to see. Notice how the author of *Cows in the Parlor* uses words and photos together in the page at the right.

The parlor in a dairy barn is not a pretty living room. It is the room where the cows are milked.

When Maggie comes in to the parlor, her udder is firm and full of milk. She stands in a small pen, or stanchion, and the gates are closed so that she can't leave until she has been milked. Every time she is milked, her udder is cleaned and all the dirt is washed off.

Farmers used to milk their cows by hand into a bucket. That took a long time. Now there are automatic milking machines to make the job quicker and easier

Are We There Yet? **25**

Photo essays are nonfiction. The words give you facts about a topic.

The photos help explain the facts. They make you feel like an eyewitness to the place and events the writer is describing.

Find Photo Essays

Look for photo essays, such as the three shown below, in your classroom or school library. Choose at least three photo essays that deal with subjects that interest you.

Hippos
by Marianne Johnston

Hippos in their African habitats

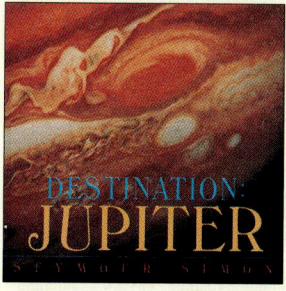

Destination: Jupiter
by Seymour Simon

Jupiter and its moons as seen from the space probes Galileo, Voyager 1, and Voyager 2

Our Baby from China
by Nancy D'Antonio

A baby adopted in China at home with her new parents in the United States

Read and Think

Read the books you chose. As you read, think:

• How does each photo help tell the story?

• How do the words and photos work together to describe events or explain information?

• Are there any photos that you think aren't needed? Which ones and why?

Share

Share your favorite photo essay with a classmate. Explain what you like about the photos and how they work together with the words to explain, entertain, or describe. Then plan a photo essay of your own. Do some research on your topic. Then start planning. For each page of your photo essay, write a sentence or two about the topic. In a box above the writing, sketch or describe the photo that should appear there. Remember that the photos should give important information and make readers feel like they are eyewitnesses to the action.

Reader Response

1. Think About the Theme

How can visits to other times and other places make our lives better? How would Poppy answer this question after her visit to Great-Grandma May's farm? What did you learn by reading about Charlie Riddle's farm? Write the answers to these questions.

2. Ask a Question

Poppy learns about what life was like for her ancestors. Imagine that you were in Poppy's place. What else would you like to know about life on the farm or about the buffalo that once roamed the prairie? Write a list of questions.

3. Use New Vocabulary

What new words did you learn from these selections? Make a list and check their meanings. Then divide the words into groups. Write a heading for each group of words, such as Words That Describe Dairy Farms, Words That Tell About the Past. Write a paragraph for each heading, using the words listed under that heading.

4. Make Connections

Imagine that you could visit the places in the selections. Which place would you rather visit and why? Write your answers.

5. Analyze

In *Cows in the Parlor* the author describes a typical day for dairy farmer Charlie Riddle. Look through the selection. What traits, such as patience and kindness, would you need to be a good dairy farmer? Write a short description of a good dairy farmer.